Going Camping

by Carol Pugliano
illustrated by Mark Reihill

I had been waiting to go
camping for a long time!
At last the day had come.
We were going to camp out in
the woods!

"Come here," said Mom. She felt my forehead.

"Honey, you feel warm," said Mom. "I'm afraid you can't go camping today."

"But, Mom," I said, "I feel fine."

"Sorry," said Mom. "We must stay home."

I felt very sad, and a little mad, too. I wanted to go camping. But I guess I did feel a bit sick.

"I have an idea," said Dad. "Let's bring the camp-out inside! We'll have a camp-*in*. Does that sound good?"

"Yes, it does!" I shouted.

We set up our tent in the
living room. We put our
sleeping bags in the tent.

"We can toast these
marshmallows," Mom said.

"Let's tell stories with the lights
out!" I said.

Our camp-*in* was the best
camping trip ever!